*Let the Ice Speak*

# *Let the Ice Speak*

POEMS BY
*Wendy Barker*

ITHACA HOUSE BOOKS

The Greenfield Review Press
Greenfield Center, NY

*Also by the author:*

*Winter Chickens and Other Poems*
*Lunacy of Light: Emily Dickinson and the Experience of Metaphor*

## Acknowledgments

I am grateful to the editors of the following journals, in which some of the poems in this manuscript appear, at times in slightly different versions or with different titles:

*The American Scholar:* "For Want of Dolls," "Requiescat, for My Father"
*California Quarterly:* "Playing the Game of Statues," "The Freezer in the House"
*Calyx:* "Persephone's Version"
*Chomo Uri:* "My Father's Living Room"
*Concho River Review:* "Baptism"
*Crosscurrents:* "Why We Went to the Ocean"
*Imagine: International Chicano Poetry Journal:* "Dancing Lessons," "My Parents, in That Light"
*Nimrod:* "Father's Fish"
*Passages North:* "Once More, Squam Lake"
*Poetry:* "Black Sheep, White Stars," "From the Attic at Thornfield," "Giving Up the Dead," "Identifying Things"
*Prairie Schooner:* "14th Spring"
*Southern Poetry Review:* "Heat, Letting Go"
*Tar River Poetry:* "My Mother's Sewing Machine"

"Black Sheep, White Stars" has also appeared in *Crossing the River: Poets of the Western United States*, ed. Ray Gonzalez. "Identifying Things" appears in *Poets Respond to AIDS*, ed. Michael Klein, and in the 1989 edition of *Anthology of Magazine Verse & Yearbook of American Poetry*, ed. Alan F. Pater.

I am especially grateful to the National Endowment for the Arts for a creative writing fellowship in poetry.

The friends who have helped with this manuscript know who they are and will continue to know my deepest gratitude.

© 1991 Wendy Barker
ISBN 0-87886-134-3

Library of Congress 90-83509

First Edition
All Rights Reserved

Ithaca House Books
The Greenfield Review Press
2 Middle Grove Road
Greenfield Center, N.Y. 12833

# Contents

## I  The Freezer in the House

| | |
|---|---|
| Baptism | 3 |
| Playing Witches at Recess | 4 |
| Playing the Game of Statues | 6 |
| Dancing Lessons | 8 |
| My Father's Living Room | 9 |
| My Parents, in That Light | 10 |
| The Freezer in the House | 11 |
| My Mother's Sewing Machine | 13 |
| Black Sheep, White Stars | 15 |
| Why We Went to the Ocean | 17 |

## II  Alternate Versions

| | |
|---|---|
| Snow White's Father's Second Wife's Tale | 21 |
| From the Attic at Thornfield | 23 |
| Persephone's Version | 26 |
| On Climbing Trees, for Louisa May Alcott | 28 |
| For Want of Dolls | 31 |
| Snow White at the Convention Finds the Bear | 34 |

## III  Sounding Dreams

| | |
|---|---|
| Heat, Letting Go | 41 |
| Sounding Dreams | 43 |
| Hurricane Warnings | 45 |
| Your 50th, What Cake | 47 |
| 14th Spring | 49 |
| Summer Time | 52 |
| Going Back, Coming Home | 54 |
| Once More, Squam Lake | 56 |
| Identifying Things | 57 |

## IV  Requiescat

| | |
|---|---|
| Father's Fish | 61 |
| Trying To | 63 |
| Requiescat, for My Father | 65 |
| Giving Up the Dead | 68 |

*For my mother,
Pamela Dodwell Bean,*

*in memory of my father,
George Clarke Bean*

*I*

*The Freezer in the House*

## *Baptism*

Light dim as the crumbled leather
of old books, and Granny next to me
leaning down with her smell of lime cologne,
finger moving across the small black shapes.
She pointed to the clusters in their tidy lines,
barely stopping under each one, as the minister
kept on talking. My baby sister slept
as he held her, no one else
seemed to breathe.
                      But Granny's finger led
my eyes on and on, back and forth, down the page,
and then I saw: she reached *the* at the same time
the minister said *the*, and it happened again,
two lines down, and there were *the*'s everywhere
on those pages—"even unto *the* end of *the* world,"
her finger moved as he said the words
out loud, "*the* kingdom, and *the* power,
and *the* glory," naming.

## Playing Witches at Recess

When we had recess at Encanto Elementary
the girls divided in teams.
                      Ours would run
behind the pyracantha, berries all red on the outside,
but inside, gold as pumpkins, and we'd scream
as the Fairies flitted by, practiced
their dancing, leaping, arabesques.
Long hair bounced and fell on their necks
the way it was supposed to
and their voices never made the teachers mad.
Scratchy runners of Bermuda grass
never caught in their white socks
with scalloped edges.

But we Witches had power.
Saddle shoes scraped and stained
by winter lawns, one braid fatter than the other,
we held the talisman we all desired,
and we never let them get it.
My English granny had sent for Christmas
a leather diary smaller than a Hershey bar,
blue paper, gold edges, ribbon for a marker.
Flipping the pages made a sound like wind,
showed the days, months divided into squares
clean as the Arizona sky after a rain.

And when we flung out over our shoulders
a chant of Saturdays and Thursdays and October
the 31st crossed with the 3rd of July, we knew
we had it all over them,
that not even their skill at ballet or tap
could combat what we learned
from fingering those blank
pages of the year, from saying their names.
Maybe we knew even then we were tracing
steps to the longest dance of all:
neither curses nor blessings, only
the ways we would decide, fill in the days.

## *Playing the Game of Statues*

Whirling and whirling as the Tucson sun
curled down, we turned so dizzy
the purple mountains would set
firm in a wide stripe dividing the haze
of gray roofs from red sky
until, having spun ourselves
out of orbit like spent tops,
we fell frozen until the one who was It
gave orders, told us to *move*.
And move we did, a frenzy of leaping,
skating, arcing our backs for the high
dive and then letting go, over and over,
to land—*stop*—on the high wire
right there on the Bermuda grass
beneath our bare feet.

    At the Galleria
dell'Accademia in Firenze, Michelangelo's
Four Slaves are still trying to separate
sinewy arms from the bulk of marble.
The David appears at the precise moment
he has become who he will be,
his head turned to one side, while we
circle around him, circle and stare
at such polished stasis, at the perfect
veins of his ankles.

How the rest of the body follows
the crisis of an instant—a freak pose
on an Arizona night
when the clouds boiled in the colors
of the High Renaissance Masters
and we whirled and flew and tried on other lives,
pirouetting or pitching, tight-rope-walking
for all we were worth,
still believing that, whenever you wanted,
you could always change your mind.

*Dancing Lessons*

A white shirt pressed his shoulders
as he taught me how to let my hand rest
in his. "A good dancer
never feels heavy in her partner's
arms," he said, so I worked
at keeping my palm a little distant

while my father's arm held my back.
"You must anticipate your partner's
next move, he should feel as if you're part
of him, always let him lead," he advised
as he dipped and toed, looking off
somewhere beyond my head.

I stumbled backward around the room
trying to keep in line
with the tidy circles he made
avoiding the green chair,
the converted player piano, my sisters' toys.
I didn't mind the music, Cole Porter was okay.

But I could feel my sweat steaming
like the dishwater my mother stood over,
her red wool shirt
above the suds, the clatter.
And as the silver jangled
offbeat in the drainer

I dreamed of climbing up to the roof.
Might be hard to dance on sloped shingles,
but there'd be night air,
maybe a breeze, my body could breathe.

## My Father's Living Room

Evening papers
crinkled in his lap,
his hands were clean,
nails trimmed short, his signet ring
had no initial.
I read the headlines from the floor,
trying to see inside, squinting to read
the little letters under the thick ones.
He turned the pages slowly.

"Don't bother your father," my mother
whispered. I learned not to. I practiced
quiet, practiced over and over
scales of silences,
learning as long as I didn't
startle him,
I could make my move
when the paper came down.

As we talked I would shiver
from holding in my words,
from not letting them out
too loudly,
from holding my ribs
close as piano keys
so I could sound
his fears.

## My Parents, in That Light

I see them in that yellow glow
of evening living rooms, beige linen
shades erasing shadow.
In that light

every thought could be curtained
among the well-upholstered arms of chairs,
easy greens and golds,
no colors allowed that might disturb

mellow illusions after dark.
When dinner would be exactly ripe was the question
asked and reasked in air thick
with the smell of lamb chops broiling.

Dinner was, after all, a matter
of proper timing, carrying
china plates, and thorough chewing.
They worked hard to digest the day,

trying not to remember
all those other dinners
when anger had jangled the plates,
when the talk would have carved the beef.

So they munched peas, mentioned
the dogs' new vet, spoke of the men
who every month pruned the natal plum.
After dinner, a return to chairs,

magazines, glossy, slick
as fat hardening in the pan.

## The Freezer in the House

Shelled peas shone on the table
the creamy satin of my grandmother's
wedding dress.
                After my parents
boiled them, they wrinkled like our fingers
when we'd been in the bath too long,
and they turned dark, dark as the shadows
under the leaves of the mulberry trees.
My mother and father scooped them into waxy white boxes,
piled them in the great white chest in the kitchen
closed tight with a silvery handle.

I'd spring on top of that freezer,
thump its slick white front with the heels of my sandals,
suck a lime popsicle pulled from its smoky depths
white as the clouds over the Rincon Mountains.
I asked my mother questions while she sliced carrots,
how to keep the boy with the plaid shirts
from teasing, how did it feel to have a baby.

When I'd licked clean the popsicle stick
and Mom said I should go outside
I biked three blocks down to Sandy Davison's.
Some days we sat out front in our bathing suits
with a tube of Prell shampoo and two razors
and practiced shaving our legs
in her little sister's inflatable pool.
The Davisons didn't have a freezer, didn't fuss
about food, they worked for the Phone Company,
belonged to the union. Sandy fixed their dinners.

Sometimes I stayed for canned corn and spaghetti,
except for the times Mr. Davison came home
with a face the color of muddy beets,
pulled his belt through the loops of his jeans,
and Sandy warned me, run, run while you can,
you can still get out, run out the back door.
I'd run as fast as I could
out to the leaves that spiralled and clung to the sky

but I took the back way home, through
acres of desert nobody had built on yet,
through creosote, palo verde trees, and I pulled
the leaves into my fingers, let them spring
into place on the branches
before I picked up the pace, headed
straight for home, hunger opening
a flat white box, empty inside.

## My Mother's Sewing Machine

The rising whine and steady
freight train roar
of her sewing machine needle's bite

took the pale gray buds
that lined my bedroom
walls and ripped them, tossed

them on the table behind
her sewing machine,
behind piles of cut-out body parts,

arms, chests, waists, great
circular or gathered skirts,
heavy as tents. On the fabric

she sewed red rick rack, rows
and rows of glittering
purple braid, all

the brilliance my father
insisted she strip
from the living room walls.

If she couldn't dash
color over the rooms
of her house, she would drape

herself and her daughters
in her own designs.
She made sure that under

the crackling dazzle of those dresses
no one would hear our silences,
no one would know

that the pressure of my mother's foot
on the pedal of her sewing machine
all but split the house.

## Black Sheep, White Stars

He'd appear like a bird
that wanders into a place
on its way between two continents.
Surrounded by houses
that sopped up sparkle like sponges
he'd roll out of a '47 black Cadillac

and wave a bottle of rum
shimmering in the sun like amber.
"Pam, darling," he'd call to my mother,
his voice so raucous
Mrs. Simonitch next door
would move one slat of her Venetian blinds.

His toes pushed from limp *huaraches*
and he grinned as if he knew
just how much acid
the sight of him
shadow-bearded, yellow under the arms,
produced in my father's stomach.

When he talked
our windows grew arches, opened doors
onto courtyards, lemon trees, parrots,
we could hear the rustling of green feathers,
the chirrings and cawings of orange birds.
Small on the sofa I said

"Let me come live with you,"
something in my lungs knowing
that in a place named Jlayacapan
people might swallow drinks
the colors of bougainvillea
and move at night

to music that had never heard
of a metronome.
And when Uncle Dick and his friend Pedro
sat me between them
on the Cadillac's dusty front seat
to watch *High Society* at the Frontier Drive In,

I held myself taut and sweaty, dreaming stars
thicker than sugar on oatmeal,
stars farther than heaven,
stars and hibiscus and mangoes
that could cluster around a life
as long as a laugh.

## Why We Went to the Ocean

That screen door slammed on too much silence.
In the car we carried it with us.
It was Daddy who muttered and fussed
about the luggage, but only to Mom
when we weren't around, so all we knew
were the great sighs, my mother's solicitous
gestures, suggestions for where to fit
the big brown bag, the box with the extra towels.
He would never be able to get it all in.

My mother kept us quiet,
hissing to the back seat.
He needed quiet to drive. The roads
were harder then, two lanes, tricky
to pass, to keep your own speed.
The heat blew in from the windows,
mixed with our father's smoke, the smoke
from the Benson and Hedges that thickened
and stopped the air.

The desert stuck in my eyes
a great brown thorny silence
until we climbed up the mountains
before San Diego and the green
began its small damp murmurings.
We could stop for lunch, walk
around, find pine needles bundled
like tiny brooms, like the wire
brushes drummers use.

From then on the roads were wider.
From then on we stretched as tall as we could
from the back seat, waiting for that first
glimpse of the long breath
of blue stretching out beyond
the horizon, and it was downhill then,
as we sang out *the sea, the sea*,
and there it was, we could run
along its slapping hard breathing
body, we could laugh as loud as we
ever wanted because the ocean
had the loudest voice in the whole world.

# II

*Alternate Versions*

## Snow White's Father's Second Wife's Tale

The stories leave out the fact
that Snow White's mother and I
were sisters. That when she died
her husband the King
and I both wept.

I had never thought about
which of us was the more beautiful,
it was always the two of us, riding
bareback over the fields,
she would cling to me,

her white breath on my neck.
We thought we were lucky:
two princes, one
for each. But our husbands
were different as snow, fire,

and roses—white roses,
red. I still miss him. Running
through wide fields, the tall
grasses whispering
over our legs—midnights

on a blanket in the forest, the moon
pulling us, reflecting us,
until there was nothing we didn't
know about each other,
until we forgot who was who.

They never told me how he died.
My sister's child came,
white as new sheets,
and then my sister died.
I don't know why

the King insisted we marry—
he wouldn't lie with me
outside in the night,
he said the leaves were damp,
the moss would stain. Why couldn't

I lie still in the pillows?
He stopped coming to me altogether.
I moved into the tower.
I am what happens
when you don't die young.

*From the Attic at Thornfield*

She did not want to burn
down the house because
she was in love with fire.

It was never that.
It was because of the closed
doors, the straight walls

that stopped any long breathing,
that told her, when she tried
to laugh, to stop.

And the chairs, the chairs
slim and delicate,
lined against the edge

of a room, lap sideways
to lap, no one facing.
Even the windows looking out

felt too slick and hard
to her fingers, nothing open
about them. How did she know

that what she saw
outside was really there?
That the hedges were any more

yielding than a locked door?
And the stones rose in walls so high,
so thick, she had never found

the way out.
                In the first delicate
lickings of flame, the lovely

leafings of orange, yellow,
the prickings and twinings
of the snapping noises,

she could hear voices,
the click of new tongues,
the lap of loud breathing,

and she knew
that as the roar began,
with its great wind, blackness,

red over brightest red, flames
that took over the sky,
she knew she did love it

now, it was all
she had ever loved,
this sweet terror

that raced its own body
together with hers
over the terraces, the gardens,

out to the orchards, the hills,
its blazing voice
finally loud enough,

that the only way it would ever stop
would be when it had spoken
to everything it could find,

and there would be,
for the first time,
nothing left, nothing

left to say.

*Persephone's Version*

My mother never
understood how, after that first time
(when the earth cracked and the blackness,
like a magnet,

dragged my feet down to the ore)
how after that, I went by myself, how
every October the pears rotting on the ground
blocked the way down, how

I burrowed under the brown fruit,
found my way, tunnelling through loam
past bedrock, drawing nearer and nearer
to the fire. In the light of flame

veins of silver, clots of gold
fed my eyes,
my hands glowed scarlet
as I held them toward the hearth.

I never could explain him to my mother,
how I set up my own forge,
had my own hammer, tongs, built
circlets of rubies, diamonds, topaz.

He didn't nag like Apollo,
always saying "Look at me, look
up, look into my eyes when you
speak." I could carve all day.

Neither my mother nor her
brother ever understood
I went because I wanted to,
year after year. They never knew

that was how I was able
to return each April
to find Narcissus, and to feed
my brilliance to the breeze.

## On Climbing Trees, For Louisa May Alcott

Then Jo and Meg . . . set forth the supper on the grass. . . . the lads were not required to sit at table . . . freedom being the sauce best beloved by the boyish soul. They availed themselves of the rare privilege to the fullest extent . . . and apple turnovers roosted in the trees like a new style of bird. . . .

— *Little Women*

1.
In first grade the sun poured
onto the rough paper
flecked with embedded
slivers of pine.

The teacher bent
over our desks, told us to make
three dots in a vertical row,
guides to keep

our letters on the right lines.
She walked around the room.
My dots grew, my pencil drew
spirals, vines, twining

until she stopped at my desk
and said to erase
all that. She would tell us
what to do next.

2.
Too tall in the fourth grade
to be the heroine
of the Brownie play,
I was turned into

a tree, brown crepe
paper wound from my feet
to my glasses, arms
ordered to stay

upright for the whole thing.
I had my cues: when the star
of the show tripped in
with her basket

my branches were to wave,
and when she asked if I had seen
the Brownies, I was to say
in a wooden voice, *no, no.*

3.
A small tree growing from one
point in the dry ground,
my father had nursed
his rhus lancea,

and our three-month-old German Shepherd
bit it off at the root.
                        Years later
I watched my three-year-old

son rustling its highest leaves—
in a dozen years it had grown
multiple trunks after its early pruning,
top branches lifting

over the Phoenix Mountains' caliche.
My father walked around on the ground
under his tree, shot dozens
of pictures.

In them our boy dangles
from a top branch, his chubby chin
sure, calm. He has climbed that far
up my father's tree.

4.

I am surrounded by live oaks. Small
Texas madrones, leaves that turn
golden in November, quiver in wind.
I never did

learn to climb a tree.
I press my cheek against the bark
of one of the old oaks, lean
against a splintering

cedar, my son's favorite
for climbing. In the crotches
of some of the oaks,
Virginia creeper, wild grape

twine around the hard crusts
of the bark, spiralling, gleaming
as they redden, even
as the light fades.

*For Want of Dolls*

1.
A woman bends
over a blanket she opens
to offer a gift: Peruvian

dolls for the dead.
Formed from shreds, figures shaped
like family, friends, made

to keep the dead from loneliness.
Their yarn mouths grin
wide ovals, loose braids drift

down long skirts, the weave
ravelling, threads dropped
from the warp.

Some of the dolls hold
little ones, babies, faces
pale as the shells of eggs.

One lies on her back, swollen belly
covered with a tapestry of gold, red.
Three figures lean over her

as the baby emerges.
I gather the dolls in a row
in my room. Silent

color of berries,
doves, of rings
inside trees.

2.

Six years old, Phoenix
subdivision too new for trees,
too hot for flowers, I craved

the Story Book Dolls at the dime store,
full skirts that rustled
like petals pressed

into cardboard and cellophane boxes.
Dolls named after stories I read
in my room with the blinds

drawn from the sun, from the square yard
outside, bare except for the oleander,
castor beans we were told

never to touch with our mouths.
I saved my nickels
for months, but all I could buy

was a plain doll, short skirt,
not someone from a book,
Snow White, Sleeping

Beauty cost too much, their velvet
and lace, coiled hair, shining
crowns. I wanted them

to bloom in a row over my bed,
their wide skirts, petticoats
ruffling the bare wall.

3.

I remember in France, driving to Chartres,
how the cathedral
lifts the valley around it. I remember

our eyes rising to portals
where saints are gathered
in rows, where stone

has been carved into lace, stories
for people who couldn't read.
And I remember how we entered

in silence the vault of light
and faced the rose
window, its great round

ringing circles within
circles
       where doves wing

down to the mother
offering her child,
pale, oval faces blooming.

## Snow White at the Convention Finds the Bear

> Snow White and Rose Red were going to run away, but they . . . stopped, and when the bear came up to them his rough coat suddenly fell off, and there stood a tall man, dressed entirely in gold. . . .
>
> —The Brothers Grimm

1.
In the chromium palace of words,
the convention hotel,
she thought he would never come.
Sleek stairs, escalators running
like rivers of glass, the potted
palms lifting manicured hands
toward the quiet, well-mannered
ceiling that spoke only in hushed
tones: *would you like, of course,
yes, we can take care of it
for you.*
            And in the elevator,
rising above restaurants, gift shops with displays
of earrings, paperbacks for insomniac nights,
she rose to the floor of her room, gray carpeted,
pad, pad, hush, on the carpet, the bags
carried for her, a quick click of the door
into her room: gray, white, a bit of coral, chintz
on the chairs, sweet air of expensive
soap clinging to the towels. Soon
there would be foam
in the bath.

2.
It happened downstairs: great
roar from the revolving doors,
arms outstretched toward her,
her name, her name, echoing in the chrome
lobby, and the wild
arms round her, his mouth telling
her what none of the meetings all day
ever could. And everyone watching,
*who is he, who is he*, with his
great beard, his gleaming
eyes, his huge shoulders and arms
around her so she could rest
like a pattern in the tapestry of his coat,
she could dance like a ballerina
on the center of his stage.
                                              She would never leave
the rough weave of his fur, the warm gray
silk of his silent belly.

3.
He refused to stay in the room.
Fussed. No fish in the bath.
He sulked, began to roar. Finally
she had to let him out, although
he knocked over the spindly-legged
tables in the halls. They had to go down by
the stairs.
                        The worst of it was that she began
to forget how to speak. His huge knees
were enough, his shagginess, the slow
coral of his wet tongue.
She found places she'd never
explored. They tried the roof, plenty of room
for him up there, no lines of chairs

crowding the air the way they did downstairs
in the meeting rooms, up here it was
all air, a wind through his fur,
and down below, the streets
like rivers, the cars like fish, his arms
almost long enough to reach
that far down.

4.

And then, on the last day,
when she knew she must go to at least one meeting,
he refused to be left, insisted she take him.
How would they fit? He would take up
five chairs, at least. And she,
she had forgotten how to talk.

                        When they arrived
the rows of chrome chairs were filled,
everyone faced the lectern, the mike,
the speaker's small glass of water.
No one saw them come in.
He stood, at the back, quiet, for once.
She was amazed, grateful.
She took a couple of notes.
She could feel
his breath, his fur, his heavy
presence. She listened.
She forgot him.

5.

There were no signs of him
in the halls, nothing knocked over.
But on the escalator down to the lobby
with old friends, laughing,
making plans for dinner, maybe red snapper, she saw

someone gleaming through the haze of tweed.
He came right up to her, reached for her arm,
and they moved off, whispering, they had
everything to say to each other—
his crown hidden in a thicket of
brown hair, just a glimpse of his coral tongue—
as they slid
into a slow dance, his thigh
moving between hers.
                        On and on
they danced through every floor, up
to the roof and down again, around
the lobby one more time, then
right on out through the glass
and chrome revolving doors, where
the streets swam silver, leaping with salmon.

*III*

*Sounding Dreams*

*Heat, Letting Go*
                    (for Larry)

You held on to your rage
the way the heat held
this year, kept
the leaves in thrall,
unnatural green on the trees
all October, November.
There was no moving through it.
Heavy air, it wouldn't say
what it wanted. The smallest jobs
were more than I could bear.
Newspapers the dogs had strewn
across the field
stayed where they were,
and the dogs found more, a neighbor's
slipper, a garden glove.
Under the grasses
the trash grew.

               Until the day I watched
your eyes turn and you saw it, for the first time.
Named it, your rage.

               It was only
a coincidence that the heat turned then,
the nights chilled so that sleep was again
an easy affair with blankets,
as the sumacs, the Spanish oaks
flamed your fury, gloried in your raging,
the crisp air flaming until even the grasses
turned burgundy in the wind,

and we lived in a red land that said,
*here it is, now, take it, take it,*
and we knew that very soon
we would be able to see
even the tiniest twigs,
the shapes of everything underlying color,
the long thorns of the sweet acacia,
the small bare swelling where
the leaf end dropped.

## Sounding Dreams

The sound a guitar makes
in a room where no one knows
what to say.

Another oatmeal carton empty,
into the trash with yesterday's papers.
Time was we'd have saved it
for a drum, or cut a mouth
below eyebrows of yellow wool,
black paper notes would stream out—
a boy singing.

This weekend we looked at electric guitars.
A man who had been on the road seventeen years
was selling a limited-edition Fender
for half its value, and our son
was possessed by his desire to possess
this blue and white and gold lily of a thing,
its neck stretching out a long clear solo.

We have stopped asking why
his acoustic guitar is not enough.
When dreams go beyond the words you own,
it's best not to question them.
But in the car coming home, all of us knew
that we could not afford the guitar,
that the house would be gray, shadow-
filled without its shimmering
sleekness, a way to notes
that would dazzle even the heaviest air.

Through the warm husk of the car
come voices of a choir on the radio,
singing some mass. The words don't matter,
it's their voices, their human
sound filling the empty space.
We tell our son, "Maybe sometime soon.
We'll try, we'll try, if we can."

*Hurricane Warnings*

Where is this wind that won't
blow through, that hovers
at the edge of weather
radio reports, the news. Predictions
drop brittle leaves on the roof.
We track the storm's path
on a map, collect water, decide
which room we will go to.

The satellite photo in the paper
swirls into a white breast, clouds
of milk surround a firm nipple
poised, ready for feeding.

I barely remember
nursing our son. The release
when the milk let down,
the feel of the fluid pulling
from some hot core, as if drawing
the whole body, the body swollen
beyond itself until it entered
the child, feeding.

When I was too tired the milk
wouldn't come. We learned
to wait. His patient
sucking as I sat quiet, looking
out the window at the camphor trees
merged in fog, and then, there
it was, the hot sting, the flow,
and his eyes glazed.

Now in the mornings when we pull
the car up to school
he opens the door in a tall
breeze of legs, shoulders, and is gone
into the crowd of kids
gathering before the bell.
The storm swirls around us.
We watch bands of dark clouds
move the sky, drop a little rain,
a little wind.

There are times I want to lift
him back into my lap,
hold him like a lanky
stuffed colt, nuzzle
his soft hair. I want him to linger
in the car, I'd like to drive on
to a zoo, a playground,
where he would say "can you see me
now, Mom, can you see," and he
would want me to say
"yes, I see you, that's great,
great, you're really climbing now."

When he leaves the car in the morning
he yanks at the handle, breaking
the air between us.
I say "bye, have a good one,"
and maybe he'll say "bye," but
if he says too much
he'll be sucked back, he must move
into that crowd
of kids gathering their own
winds that will swallow us all.

## Your 50th, What Cake
(December 10, 1988)

For the birthday you said
you'd never see. Years
back I had said (in my 19-
year-old smiling) oh yes
you will, and more, and more,
I'll see to that, for I had read
of all the good
women who kept men alive
with fresh pink
cheeks by the fire,
their dainty
nibbles. Such sweetness
could not help
but keep a man going
long after he had
decided there wasn't
much point, long after
a dream had stretched
so far off the horizon's
edge his eyes hurt
from the strain of following,
had to look down, through
half-glasses, try again
to follow the interest rates.

What cake. One friend said sweet,
sticky, the kind we never
eat any more, swirls of sugar
icing over layers
of puffed white flour.
But not your sort. Never was.

So when another friend told me
what he wanted to do,
I laughed until the sky
moved in under my heels,
moved the horizon
right next door.
Hire one of those huge
hollow cakes with a girl
inside, she'd leap right out,
pasties glistening
like strawberry glaze.
Maybe that would be all
it would take: one whiff
of such sugar
and you'd remember
that the white in your beard
is icing too, sweet, rich,
and still in the making.

## 14th Spring

We had taken winter into ourselves
for more than one season.
Shrivelled

stalks of grasses, seed
gone, our boy slamming alone
into his room,

locked. You and I
carried the weight
of the cold silence,

guilt pressing our shoulders,
*why didn't we, we could
have, we should.*

The belly learned
to live with lessened
expectation, made do

with memories of color: citron,
withered currants.
                    Nothing much

moves in winter, a pair
of cardinals, bit of red, pinky
brown, a few jays, screeching,

cheeky blue.
Now in May, the bread rises
before I'm ready.

Thumb punches down,
and the hollow
navel, dark imprint, fills,

dough belly
swelling seamless
over the bowl.

Air so light, you and I might
as well be two
of the wine-cups, poppy

mallows, spilling
over the hills
covered with yellow

composites, hundreds of seeds
held in their centers,
gold as yolks.

And our son, a lead
in the 8th grade play,
brought down the house.

At night now he leaves his door
open, talks on the phone, at dinner
laughs at our jokes.

This afternoon, you call out:
beyond the deck, slowly
through the grass pulses

a hognosed snake.
It opens a wide glistening mouth
before it is gone, a wave

of muscle in the grass,
leaving us standing, trying
to digest all this,

yet knowing
it will take seasons,
years of long summers

to travel
the lacy intricacies
of the body, the belly,

as it fills.

## Summer Time

The days swim to a slow center.
Bean vines surround

their poles, zinnias
ruffle fatter and fatter,

heads rise to a yellow peak.
There are things I had meant to do.

Lists, the rectangles of calendars,
tidy grids, expectations.

The days start
hot, grow hotter, turn dark.

At night I read, tell myself,
tomorrow, I'll wake early,

get going, get to it.
But every morning the plants

want more water, the golden-
fronted woodpecker nesting

beyond the house needs
watching when it comes

to the feeder.
And last night after we peeled

half the peaches
we brought down from Fredricksburg,

sliced them small,
juice slipping off the table,

I had to watch:
my son's aunt, bent

over the old manual
ice-cream maker, turning the crank,

foot stomping, stomping, because
our son was out there on the deck

with her, his electric guitar
and his amp plugged in,

wailing on the strings,
the two of them singing,

singing, the handle turning,
the peaches and cream thickening.

## Going Back, Coming Home

We brought our week-old son
into that pastel stucco house
in Berkeley, wrapped most days in fog,

pale threads unwinding
as the day moved on toward noon.
Now on a gray day in August

we go back with our fourteen-year-old boy,
seven years after we watched
the moving van drive off

down the hill, and we stare
at the street, our old wooden
porch, the front door.

We visit the neighbors: Sandy, at ninety,
still cultivates orchids, and Ron, up the street,
has moved into astrophysics, observes

dark matter, whatever it is we can't see
that swirls beyond the orbits of galaxies.
They are all still there.

                        Coming home,
the heat of our lives returns
in the first breath of entering.

Air conditioning turned off, bills
stacked on the desk,
newspapers coiled on a chair.

I have read that inside
the nucleus of the atom
are particles, tiny points

that, looked at from another direction, turn
into waves, the single point
loosened, changed.

I think of the knot on an oak branch
outside my bedroom window, a gnarl
I stare at trying to wake up.

Once, while working outside, I tried
to see where this bulge
lay along the line of branch,

but never could. It exists
only from one place on the bed.
We came home to the heat, relentless

pressure of the day's questions,
who will take
the old car, when will we

get to the dentist, who will
market, what time,
what time.

Until the rain let down
long blue lines that began
somewhere in the upper atmosphere

of clouds, ended in the parched
flat ground, single points rippling
puddles, spirals, waves.

## Once More, Squam Lake

The lake whitens in the hot light
of July. At Sandy Beach we see the sunfish
circling their eggs, rippling the water.
The sunfish do what they've done before,
will do again. I sit in a haze

of sisters, nieces, mothers, grandmothers.
When I was seven, Old Jane Noble was Young
Jane Noble. When I was seventeen
she was one of the mothers who knitted
argyles on the playhouse porch.

Too hot today for socks, for knitting.
But tonight the loons will yodel
and last week they counted
nine new chicks, three more than last year.
My son is learning to fish the lake.

My father will teach him
to let the line fall quietly
(only a small furrow of water moving
beyond the nylon thread),
to hear where bass live, to find the depth

of the lake. I watch from the dock,
the lake takes the planks and rocks them
backward, forward, I forget
how old I am, what year it is,
how it all matters.

## Identifying Things

Is diabetes catching, he asks,
middle school braggadocio edged
this time with something else, I can't
quite put my finger on it,
until he tells about the needle,
that kid Jamie, jabbing a needle he had picked up
on the street, punctured far into the flesh
of my son's palm.

Trouble boils a greasy steam into the air.
Whose needle, what kind, whose veins
had it entered? My son, my son, only eleven
years old and the doctor over the phone doesn't help,
his nurse says you bet, plenty to worry about,
and it's not just AIDS we'd want to run tests for,
three strains now of hepatitis, find the needle,
bring in the needle, make sure those boys
find that needle.

                Under the oaks
a new kind of bird flocks at the feeder,
I have no idea what they are, they swarm
and dart around the perches, on the ground,
they are everywhere, and outside their shrill
wheezing chokes out the drone of trucks on the interstate.

So he will teach us death, perhaps.
We will allow him the perfect death.
We will all work on dying
together, we will give him that, and maybe
it won't even happen, maybe the needle
belonged to Jamie, he's a diabetic,

maybe it was just one of his own insulin needles,
probably there is nothing in the world
to worry about, chances are slim, we mustn't
upset our boy, mustn't blow this out
of proportion.

                I can't identify
the birds. They are too streaked
for goldfinches, they could be
warblers, winter plumage, but their beaks
are a little thicker, I'm just not sure
and none of these walls
line up straight.

When the boys find the needle and take it
to the principal and you stop by school
our kid is most upset because his father
is actually seen by his friends, only nerds have
parents who enter this territory,
he will never live it down, his own father
picking him up in front of his friends,
driving him to the doctor's. Just a little needle,
the kind for pricking a finger for small
blood samples, adults always overreact.
The doctor and the nurses laugh out loud,
at home the walls rise crisp
to the ceiling where the light dances.

                      And the new birds
are pine siskins, yes, they are,
just a little yellow on the wings and tail,
it helps, it always helps when you know
what things are.

# IV

## *Requiescat*

## Father's Fish

I have seen them flop and heave
silver muscle on the boat bottom
and these were not those fish.

Rather they were feathers,
amethysts, sunsets,
clouds swirling and gleaming

in a rectangular blue world
he kept perfect: temperature,
pH, plants, clean gravel, all

perfect. And silent. Such brilliant
silences.
        Even the mouths
of the neon tetras, of the knife-narrow

black and white triangular angels
opened only the way a cry
in a dream clutches at silence,

the throat tries, strains
to be heard, aches to reach
the ears that stand

on the other side of the glass
but there is no sound, nothing.
And perhaps the ears would rather

watch, only follow with the eyes
the fishy sliverings, the tailings
and questionings round and round

in the water, and forget what it took
to keep it all going: emptying
the tubes, cleaning the white

gravel, replacing the charcoal,
never overfeeding. It may have been
too much trouble.

There is no longer an aquarium
in that house. Now
on a Northern lake I see him

bent in the boat, hands
trembling as he changes
the lure, prepares

to cast over
the lake's blue ridges,
hoping to reach

the mouths of small bass
as they shimmer
under dark rocks, cut

through dark water,
hoping their mouths will open
eye to eye with his,

yet knowing
that the only way
it will happen

will come in the sharp pull
they both hear,
silent, when the hook holds.

## Trying To

As if under this wood a spirit could rise.
Rubbing and rubbing, I am unable to leave
the smoothness of tables, the cool
surface of kitchen counters. Fingerprints
on the bathroom mirrors I wipe away.
As if everything in this house
could gleam with its own right shape.

There are things that happen everyone says
could not be helped, there was nothing
anyone could do. I am trying to believe that.
I try not to say every morning when the line
of trees sharpens the bedroom window: If only.
If only I would have, he might have.

We have now had the dividing of spoils.
He would have said it like that, with a grin.
My son keeps his last four rolls
of Stick-O-Pep lifesavers, says he will
keep them unopened in memory of Grandfather,
maybe once a year peel back the foil
and suck just one, for good luck.
The brothers-in-law own more ties
than they ever thought they wanted.
Last month we sorted the books, shipped
boxes to each of the sisters.

When I rub and rub, the refrigerator
glows like a white shrine.
The sun folds clean stripes across the bed,
the sheets lie flat, unrumpled.
The bed sits squarely in the room.
This morning I had not wanted to leave it.
I sleep with his travel alarm
by my head, his silver bookmark
digging its delicate arrow
into the meat of my book.

## Requiescat, For My Father

1.
No more travel
on this lake for now.
His boat has been stored and soon
the ice will begin to gather.
In the heaviest month
the men will come to cut the ice.
Great cubes. Lift them into the icehouse,
pile on pile, up to the roof.
Somewhere off Loon Island
his bones have been scattered.
Ashes, they call them, but
I know better. They will take a long time
to melt.

2.
Summer evenings on the screened porch,
breeze in the pines, clinking
of ice and sweet smell
of Scotch from their glasses
while we sipped
ginger ale, tried not to argue,
allowed to sit with the grownups.
I had white socks, blue barrettes
clipped over my braids
and was beginning to know
how hungry I was
for dinner.

It will be a long time
before I can hear
the jingle of ice in a glass.
I avoid groups, political
discussions, people who say
they've never been better.

3.

How many pieces of line left
at the bottom of the lake? Hooks
caught on rocks, lures
lost in the sand. And the last
great catch, eight four-pounders
he caught with Sam Howe,
a day in heaven they said,
until they found
that neither had secured
the stringer, the whole day's catch
gone back to the lake.
No story had ever been quite so funny,
and yet they had lost
the catch of their lives,
and it was my father's last.
But they'd had the day, he said.

All those soft places
under the lake, places he had only
found in the last few years,
his hair thin, silvery as the scales
of the small-mouthed bass
he had begun to learn
to bring up into the boat.
It tired him to clean them
down on the dock,
stooping over, but he wanted
to cook them for dinner.

4.

The ice is patching the lake
together, even now as I watch
cool shadows thread the fields.
We will leave the sandy bottom
alone for awhile, the tenderness
of moss on rocks.

Let the ice crust.
By June, when we take the metal pick
to the chunk of blue ice
cut from the lake and stored
under layers of clean straw
we will turn and face
the wide water that stretches
to Red Hill, to East
and West Rattlesnake Mountains,
and we will let the ice speak,
let the ice speak in the glass.

*Giving up the Dead*

1.
                    Is never easy.
Lines of folks there were, not only
moms and dads with young ones,
waiting to get in
to breathe for ten minutes
in a world so long defunct
we can't even imagine
the spaces between us.

The dinosaurs, titans before us,
lizardly mysteries, why did their time
come so suddenly, how did they go?

Their great necks
circle over our heads.
There was a time we had to crane
our necks just to look
into our fathers' faces.
We climbed the mountains of their knees,
sat quiet in their laps.

These are the largest creatures
we can imagine, old gods, great
grandfathers and grandmothers nobody
knows what happened to.

And yet when we touch their skin,
we find it soft as an old sofa,
soft as reading *Babar* in bed
before the light is turned out.

2.

The ice yesterday glazed the fields,
white glass heightening oak leaves,
thickened petals, a solid world.

Today the dogs tear
the bare dirt with their nails,
the leaves quiver after yesterday's
unanimous white, broad stretch of ice.

The trees are smaller without
all that whiteness, there is nothing
to look up to.

How the world shifts when the old
fathers are gone. We had always been
the small ones, living under the shadows
of the huge trees, the giants
among us.

Some say
dinosaurs had warm blood, were not
reptilian at all, these ancestors
of birds.

                Outside my window the tiny
chipping sparrows gather. Dozens,
sweeping the ground. Barely
visible against the cold dirt,
the dried grasses, the colors
of winter. Sometimes I forget
to look, make sure
they are still there.